Salted Ink

Mahira Khan

BookLeaf Publishing

India | USA | UK

Presentation by *BookLeaf Publishing*

Web: www.bookleafpub.com

E-mail: info@bookleafpub.com

ISBN: 978-93-5744-353-1

First edition 2022

DEDICATION

This feels like my Oscar speech. You cant see the shocked and surprised look on my face right now but its there, trust me. I shall now proceed with my speech after wiping away some tears of excitement. I'd like to take this opportunity (space) to thank my Dada (grandfather) who passed down a writing gene to my father, yes they exist, no I do not have any scientific evidence to prove it. I'd like to thank my father for passing that gene on to me and believing in me and my writing skills. Without him and his tireless efforts to not only come up with a new bedtime story every night but also include my critique and narratives in those stories, I wouldn't have been able to embrace the art of storytelling. I'd like to thank my mother for the wit and charm I seem to think i posses and some of the very dramatic movies she made me watch that helped me become the drama queen poetess that I am. I wish you could see me become the star you saw in me. I'd like to thank my baby sister, who I never called my sister because I am an only child. But it's time I acknowledged that blood doesn't make a sister, a beautiful bond like ours does. Thank you for your endless supply of love and sandwiches. Finally I'd like to thank the man who helped me wake up from my dream and finally make it a reality. Without you this book would not have happened or be seen in the window display at my favourite bookstores. You sparked this vision. Thank you Max, for endlessly inspiring me and sta duaganay dee.

Infected

I know I am infected
I am infected with a disease that has killed many
like me for centuries before me
One would think by now a cure would've been
found
That maybe the collective ache would've broken
the cycle of infections
Alas, we sit here with our deteriorating selves
Some turn to ink and tears to keep the disease
from consuming them
While others burn the pain through fire and
smoke
We can't ignore the fact that we are all victims of
love
We may not know how and when we got
infected
But every time our heartbeat utters the names
that turn us pale we are reminded we have it
There are days we embrace it with a naïve
reassurance, longing for affection
On other days we try to hide behind closed
curtains, in dark corners drowning in loud music
But this disease knows all too well how to
penetrate this façade of escapes

For it knows that secretly we desire to be
consumed by this illness
Thinking that the very thing that destroyed may
somehow have the power to heal us

Disoriented

There is a moment of disorientation when you
wake up
A moment in which you don't know who you
are, what you've done and where you're headed
A moment so purely oblivious to the elements
that you call your life
If you run to the mirror in time, you might not
even recognize the silent body staring at you,
nor the thoughts that define its identity
That is the moment I crave the most
That is the moment I wish to embrace just a little
longer
Until a day may come that I am no longer
plagued by the entities that control me and I've
run so far away from the control center that my
soul is free to become again

Underneath

Why does the best in me evade me so often?
Its like the minute I'm seen, I switch off
Can you see who I am?
Do you even want to see me?
I don't think I do
Pressure and responsibility to follow through
To be consistent in a world as demanding as this
As you read this, perhaps you're intrigued but for
how long can I hold your gaze?
And once it has passed, will I still be worthy?
The indistinct lines between the other and the
self
At what point does your alleged appraisal of me
or the lack there of determine my presence, here
and now?
I am a culmination of masks, cheap imitations of
totems I admired and they cascade past my face
Can you really be certain
Can I really be certain there is anything
underneath

Seen

As I enter an abandoned room, this desolate
place inside my psyche
I pass upon a broken mirror, glimpses of the self
begin to emerge like ruins in a windswept desert
Will you walk with me?
Will you be my witness as I pull these shards
a-whole and in a moment of lucidity, see what
I've become
As I write, a new sensation takes ahold of me
A profound feeling of being disrobed
Its exhilarating, like my skin is ablaze
You may watch and you may see my light both
blinding and warm at the same time

Banished

And while you live freely I banish myself to an
early grave
A few feet above the ground, with four posts and
sheets that cling on to every inch of willpower
that wishes to rise up from it
My bed doesn't just catch all the sheep I count at
night to forget I'm awake and you're asleep
My bed absorbs every tear and scream I've let
out in order to drown you out
If I wasn't able to show you how I ever felt,
lay in my bed and you'll dream of the nightmares
I've smiled through each night

River

Why does the river call my name in the darkness

Unknowingly it gauges my interest with a
glimmer in the mirror

It doesn't just catch my eye
It casts a spell on my aching heart that longs to
cry

Why am I running to the river on this cold eerie
night
Not a sound to be heard expect the sweet sound
of my name

****

Why do you call me here at this ungodly hour
No answer
Just a direction
It's me
I'm the reason I'm here
The wind tells me I need to become one with my
reflection

****

I could jump into my own existence and it would
cause a devastation but then release me from the
realm that decays me

****

But what about them?
Will they miss me?
Will they ever wonder?
The rain will remind them of the heart that was
bursting with questions and never any answers

They'll stop and ponder
Maybe to escape it
Maybe to capture it

****

Maybe the river is right
Maybe I belong in the skies

As they run for shelter they will remember why
you ran to me that night

******

A little discomfort and a just a little hurt
All will be settled once you've reached the edge.

Vultures

I am here
I am at your table
I am at your mercy
The council of vultures look ready
Why do they love me so?
Is it my scent, my skin or my enigmatic grin?
They must be puzzled by my lack of resistance
I am forever in awe of their constant persistence
To chase me down wherever I go
To hold me close to their arms as they come in
slow
They're tender with their claws
I am transparent with my flaws
I lie there waiting
They seem to be hesitating
Feast upon me, piece by piece
Take what you like and let my heart cease
I am ready
I am ready

Anniversary of Loss

You're going to die again tomorrow, for the third
time
The first time was hard enough but just like
groundhog day I have to relive this painfully
traumatic day every year
A truck full of toxins is about to hit me at a
speed of 220 miles per hour
I will collide with it and absorb 365 tons of pure
sadness that I'll try and wash off a ton a day but
I'll be back to square one by the time I can hope
I'm free
Alas, that's life now
Maybe one day I wont be strong enough to wash
any of it away
One day, it'll consume me and I will embrace
you again
To that day mama

Awake

To wake up each day with a soul crushing first
breath into reality
Gasping for the last seconds of a world less
consuming
Dodging the piercing rays of sun trying to creep
in through the gaps in the curtains
Avoiding sounds that beckon my name back into
the world
If I cant sleep forever can I at least pretend I'm
not awake
Can I just leave this vessel that bleeds on words?
Can I just stop for a second and the let the world
destroy me once and then forever promise to
never touch me again?

Lahore

And if I could escape for a little while
I would run to the rooftop and lay under the faint
splatter of stars across the dusty scape
The sound of azaan infusing into the warm night
sky
I'd even appreciate that smoky smell mixed with
the aroma of jasmines
Some odd fireworks and the sound of children
afraid and excited at what they've pulled off
I'd bask in the way they say my name on my soil
I'd snuggle in a huge thick blanket with huge
flowers, little aesthetic appeal but warmth from
years of beautiful memories
I'd drink some karak chai and think of everyone
I love not being a phone call, time zones and
continents away but only a few minutes drive
whenever I will
If I could sneak into your realm just for a little
while I'd hug you and say;
Lahore, you've always been mine but I am no
longer yours and it kills me to say this but we
both know its better this way for a longer while

Blocks

When I was young I was gifted a box full of
Lego blocks
I explored blocks of all shapes, sizes and colours
They all belonged to me and were mine to
explore and build a castle of dreams with
Gradually as I grew older my blocks lost their
colour, their order and gathered dust
I slowly began to lost the vital blocks and was
left with a box that was only good enough to
make a sound if shaken, merely to validate the
existence of its contents
And that was when I realized I was the box and
my life only made sound to show I existed but
on the inside I was blocks away form collapsing

Night Cityscape

Night cityscape
Glimmering lights
As if they're trying to tell me I'm not alone
But I am
I sit here alone, staring at you
But you're not alone
We all just stare at you alone
You are seen collectively by all of us,
individually
We're glorifying a death we have not met as if
that's the way out
But we both know its not so why is that the only
option you're showing me?
Why am I praying for a thunderstorm?
Maybe so it can drown the sounds of the storm I
cant contain inside me
Please rumble
Please roar so I can drown my battles in your
glory
I want you to show me I'm not alone
Every inch of you is inhabited
Maybe even more than you might have wanted
But then why are we all alone?

Run

The questions have settled in her eyes
The dark circles, ink spills from heavy words
She's feeling them seep into her stream of
consciousness
Like beats
Tiny beats throbbing at her heart
each one with a question
Where is this going?
Did you make it?
Will you make it?
Run

Paris

Oh darling we had Paris
But more than Paris, we had regrets
They had tongues
We had eyes
We could see
What they wouldn't dare to speak
But we knew what they felt about us
And now we feel like we were waltz to their
beats
Maybe
Maybe because our tune was out of sync?
Was it lifetimes ago when I felt that touch on my
skin
Oh it felt like a sin
But a sin I wish to feel
And be with again
The night is young and the nightmares approach
Will we make love or draw blood?

Hush

The evil that lurks in clouds and clusters around
me float very close to igniting my heart
But I know if I speak of them, I allow them to
exist in narratives
And once you've opened the door to a
conversation you've envisioned but never spoken
of
You've invited them into the realm of your
reality

She's Still Next Door

You're still next door
You're in bed
You're watching a crime documentary
Maybe you're laughing and talking to your best
friend like you do every night
I'm crying but it's ok
My biggest fear is not getting enough A's in O
levels
My walls are still pink
The grass is still green
The world hasn't touched me yet
I haven't cut myself yet
He hasn't walked into my life
I don't listen to sad songs
I'm still listening to Avril Lavigne
I love my converse collection
I don't know what pain truly means
The only pain I know is the pain when you come
home late
I don't know boys
I don't even know just how deeply the wrong
one can penetrate and damage you
When I see rain, I only see rain

I don't know ways to release a pain I haven't felt
yet
My fears are limited to my school yard
I don't know what life has planned for me
All I know is if I turn the golden knob you'll be
on the other side
And any tear I shed will be soaked in your heart
and not a burden I will ever need to carry alone
Yes
When I close my eyes
I'm still in my bed
And you're still next door

Peace

When did the misunderstood become the
monsters
When did their tears become your poison
When did mercy pertain to your goodness and
banishment become their fate
What storms they carry and can not contain
What pain they Band-Aid but can not escape
Thirsty for kindness their hearts will bleed
Until a thousand pricks lead to the final scene
Rest my beloved you have felt more than they
have seen
Let not the world dissuade you from tasting the
nectar of peace

Hunted

I am here again, in flesh and blood
Ready for you to claim your trophy
The prize for the coveted hunt
You games are apparent and your intentions are
loud
I am not afraid of the gun, the barrel or even the
fallen crown
I do not see death as your gun aims for my heart
I see love in the eyes that once held this gun
with the same nuance and attention as when they
held my breath
I know that love and pain have been
synonymous
So, what I feel in my final moments is exactly
how I was meant to feel from the moment I let
you pass through the gates
You are an eccentric artist and I am the prey that
will become art once you pull the trigger
Through taxidermy you will immortalize my
pain on your wall
I will look to others like myself and we will
smile at our unfortunate yet imminent fall
The walls hold stories of your countless
exhibitions

Our tears hold tales of our individual
annexations
I get on my knees and stare at you
You bring the gun closer and smile at me
And this is how it's going to end

Victory Song

My heart explodes with warm joy
It asks me, about this mysterious boy
Can we trust him and his eyes that hold galaxies
full of possibilities within them
I laugh and wonder if I am hallucinating when I
gaze upon this luminous gem
Have I finally found the key that can unlock this
cage of swarming doubts
Maybe these lands will be lush again and this
will be the end of all my droughts
Before I can answer, hope takes my hand and we
dance in a majestic hall to La Vita E' Rosa
It leans in and whispers in my ear, don't be
afraid to come closer my dear
I gaze into its eyes and see everything he has
made me feel
I pray, that hope finds those who believe they
have no more left
I have found my red
In this world of greys and dread
My journey to healing may still be long
But your embrace will be my victory song

Rising

The sun is rising after a nightfall of many years
Erasing the landscape of nights full of terrors
and tears
There's a soft revolution brewing inside my
chamber of fears
With every passing day I find myself shedding
these ghastly layers
I can see the demons abandoning their post
And a glimmering ray lighting up the coast
You've set my life on a brand new course
Bringing me glad tidings with your enigmatic
force
The rivers are running
The bees are humming
My heart may finally beat again
I can stand at the shore and feel the warm waters
at my feet again

Not Alone

Maybe you're hiding behind a exuberant display
window
Behind all the glittering neon lights and pink
flamingos
There's a broken heart at play
Wondering if these scars will fade or see another
day
Roll up your sleeves and wear them with pride
Rise from the darkness with your valiant stride
You've come so far, now don't lose hope
I know life matters and emotions are a slippery
slope
But with each day we come out of a conquered
fight
Our broken spirits can rise from these turbulent
tides
Give it you heart, your blood and soul
Rest assured, you are not on this path alone